Mastering ChatGPT for Success

Max Revene

Contents

1. Chapter 1: Introduction to ChatGPT   1

2. Chapter 2: Using ChatGPT for Success   5

3. Chapter 3: Strategic Planning with ChatGPT   8

4. Chapter 4: Business Correspondence and Communication with Chatgpt   12

5. Chapter 5: Research and Education through ChatGPT   14

6. Chapter 6: Personalized Learning Experience with ChatGPT   18

7. Chapter 7: Ethical Considerations in Educational Use of ChatGPT   23

8. Chapter 8: Utilizing ChatGPT in Research   28

9. Chapter 9: Critical Evaluation of Content Generated by ChatGPT   32

10. Chapter 10: Legal Advice through ChatGPT   36

11. Chapter 11: Getting Started with ChatGPT   40

12. Chapter 12: Writing Books with ChatGPT   45

13. Chapter 13: Ethical Considerations in Using ChatGPT   49

14. Chapter 14: Safety Measures in Using ChatGPT   54

15. Chapter 15: Understanding Limitations of ChatGPT   58

16. Chapter 16: Making the Most of ChatGPT   63

17. Chapter 17: Applying ChatGPT in Customer Service   67

18. Chapter 18: Conclusion   72

Chapter 1: Introduction to ChatGPT

Understanding ChatGPT

ChatGPT is a state-of-the-art language processing AI developed by OpenAI, designed to understand and generate human-like text based on the input it receives. It's part of the GPT (Generative Pretrained Transformer) family, which has been trained on diverse internet text. ChatGPT can engage in conversations, answer questions, and provide explanations as if it were a human interlocutor.

The technology behind ChatGPT involves machine learning algorithms that have digested vast amounts of text data. By identifying patterns in this data, the model learns to predict what word should come next in a sentence given all the previous words. This predictive capability allows it to generate coherent and contextually relevant responses.

One of the most remarkable aspects of ChatGPT is its versatility. It can be employed across various industries for tasks such as customer service automation, content creation, language translation, and even tutoring. For instance, in customer service, ChatGPT can handle routine inquiries without human intervention, allowing human agents to focus on more complex issues.

However, understanding ChatGPT also means recognizing its limitations as an AI tool. While it can simulate conversation effectively, it does not possess understanding or consciousness. Its responses are based on patterns rather than comprehension. This distinction is crucial when evaluating its suitability for certain tasks—especially those requiring deep understanding or ethical judgment.

Capabilities and Limitations of ChatGPT

ChatGPT's capabilities are extensive but not boundless. On one hand, it excels at generating human-like text across various topics and styles with impressive coherence and relevance. Its ability to maintain context over a series of exchanges makes it particularly useful for applications like virtual assistants or interactive storytelling.

In creative domains such as writing fiction or poetry, ChatGPT can serve as a collaborative tool that helps overcome writer's block by suggesting ideas or composing drafts that authors can refine. In education, its capacity to tailor explanations to different levels of complexity makes it an invaluable resource for personalized learning experiences.

Moreover, businesses have harnessed ChatGPT's capabilities for enhancing productivity through automating repetitive tasks like drafting emails or generating reports. In strategic planning and budgeting processes, its ability to quickly synthesize information from various sources into coherent narratives aids decision-makers in assessing their options more efficiently.

Despite these strengths, there are notable limitations users must navigate when employing ChatGPT. The AI lacks true comprehension; thus it may produce plausible-sounding but factually incorrect information—a phenomenon known as "hallucination." Users must therefore verify any critical information provided by the model before relying on it.

Another limitation is context retention; while capable of maintaining context over short interactions better than previous models, longer dialogues may lead to loss of coherence or relevance in responses due to memory constraints inherent in current AI architectures. Furthermore, despite advancements in reducing biased outputs through improved training methods and datasets filtering processes—biases do still exist within these models due to their training on real-world data which itself contains biases.

Ethical Considerations in Using ChatGPT

The use of advanced AI like ChatGPT raises several ethical considerations that must be addressed responsibly by both developers and users alike. One primary concern is ensuring that the generated content does not perpetuate harmful stereotypes or spread misinformation—an issue compounded by the model's occasional generation of convincing yet inaccurate statements.

To mitigate these risks requires constant vigilance from developers who implement safeguards against inappropriate content generation and from users who must critically assess outputs before dissemination—particularly when used in sensitive contexts such as education where misinformation could have significant negative impacts on learners' understanding.

Privacy concerns also loom large with technologies like ChatGPT since interactions often involve processing personal data which could potentially be misused if not properly protected through robust security measures adhering strictly to privacy regulations like GDPR or HIPAA depending on jurisdictional requirements.

Moreover, there's an ongoing debate about authorship rights when AI- generated content becomes indistinguishable from human-created works—a legal gray area with implications for copyright laws currently ill-equipped to handle such complexities arising from AI contributions within creative processes.

Finally yet importantly is the consideration around job displacement; while automation through AI offers efficiency gains—it also poses risks for workforce displacement especially within roles heavily reliant upon routine cognitive tasks susceptible to automation through tools like ChatGPT which necessitates thoughtful approaches towards workforce re-skilling initiatives ensuring societal benefits outweigh potential drawbacks associated with technological progress.

Chapter 2: Using ChatGPT for Success

Enhancing Productivity with ChatGPT

In the realm of productivity, ChatGPT emerges as a formidable ally. This AI-driven tool can streamline workflows, automate mundane tasks, and facilitate decision-making processes. By integrating ChatGPT into daily operations, individuals and organizations can free up valuable time to focus on more strategic initiatives.

One of the most significant impacts of ChatGPT on productivity is its ability to handle routine inquiries and communications. For instance, customer service departments can deploy ChatGPT to manage initial customer interactions, addressing common questions or concerns before escalating more complex issues to human representatives. This not only speeds up response times but also allows customer service teams to concentrate on providing higher-quality personalized support.

Moreover, project managers can leverage ChatGPT's capabilities for task management and coordination. By interacting with the AI, they can quickly generate project plans, assign tasks based on team members' availability and expertise, and even predict potential bottlenecks using historical data analysis provided by the tool.

In research settings, ChatGPT proves invaluable in sifting through extensive databases and academic papers to extract relevant information swiftly. Researchers can engage in dialogue with the AI to refine their queries and receive summaries that would otherwise take hours to compile manually.

However, it's crucial to recognize that while ChatGPT enhances productivity significantly, it should be viewed as a complement rather than a replacement for human judgment. Users must remain vigilant in verifying the accuracy of information provided by the AI and apply critical thinking when making decisions based on its output.

Visual Designing with ChatGPT

ChatGPT's utility extends beyond text-based applications into the visual design sphere. While traditionally an area dominated by human creativity and intuition, AI now offers tools that assist designers in conceptualizing and executing their visions more efficiently. For example, graphic designers can use prompts within ChatGPT to brainstorm ideas for logos or branding elements. The AI can suggest color schemes or typographies based on industry trends or psychological associations tied to certain hues or fonts.

Additionally, designers working on user interface (UI) projects might employ ChatGPT to generate placeholder text for mockups or even provide feedback on usability aspects by simulating user interactions. Furthermore, illustrators could find inspiration through conversations with ChatGPT about various art styles or historical influences related to their work. The AI could serve as a virtual muse that helps artists overcome creative blocks by offering new perspectives or challenging existing concepts.

Chapter 3: Strategic Planning with ChatGPT

Budgeting Techniques using ChatGPT

Budgeting is a critical component of strategic planning, serving as the financial blueprint for an organization's operations. With the advent of AI tools like ChatGPT, budgeting can be transformed from a tedious, manual process into a dynamic and interactive experience. ChatGPT can assist in creating detailed budgets by providing real-time data analysis and forecasting. For instance, it can analyze historical financial data to identify trends and patterns that may influence future budgets. By inputting past expenditure and revenue figures, organizations can use ChatGPT to predict future financial scenarios with varying degrees of certainty.

Moreover, ChatGPT can help in zero-based budgeting (ZBB), where every expense must be justified for each new period. The AI can assist managers in evaluating the necessity and efficiency of each cost element by providing comparative analysis and suggesting alternatives based on organizational data.

In participatory budgeting processes, ChatGPT could facilitate collaboration among various departments. It could act as an intermediary that collects inputs from different stakeholders and consolidates them into a coherent budget proposal. This would ensure transparency and inclusivity in the budgeting process. Another innovative application is using ChatGPT for scenario planning within the budget context. Organizations often need to prepare for multiple potential futures; here, ChatGPT could simulate various economic conditions—such as changes in market demand or supply chain disruptions—and their impact on the budget.

For small businesses or startups with limited resources for dedicated financial analysts, ChatGPT serves as an invaluable tool. It can guide entrepreneurs through the creation of their initial budgets by asking relevant questions about expected income streams, cost structures, and capital expenditures. Real-world examples include startups that have used AI to optimize their cash flow management by predicting late payments or identifying unnecessary expenses. Similarly, non-profits have leveraged AI tools like ChatGPT to maximize their fund allocation towards mission-critical activities while minimizing administrative overheads.

The world of business is a complex and ever-changing landscape. To navigate it successfully, strategic planning and effective decision-making are crucial. In this chapter, we will explore how ChatGPT can be a valuable tool in these processes, providing insights and enhancing productivity. In today's fast-paced business environment, time is of the essence.

Business leaders need to make informed decisions quickly to stay ahead of the competition. This is where ChatGPT comes into play. By leveraging its capabilities, you can analyze budgets, taxation strategies, and maximize profitability with ease. Imagine you are a finance manager for a multinational corporation. You have been tasked with creating a strategic plan for the upcoming fiscal year. Instead of spending hours poring over spreadsheets and financial reports alone, you decide to utilize ChatGPT as your trusted assistant. With just a few prompts, you can extract valuable insights from large datasets in no time. Chat-GPT can help you identify trends, evaluate different scenarios, and make data-driven decisions that align with your company's goals.

Let's take a look at an example transcript:

Finance Manager: "ChatGPT, analyze our current budget allocation and suggest areas where we can optimize."

ChatGPT: "Based on historical data analysis and industry benchmarks, I recommend reallocating funds from department X to department Y. This adjustment will better align resources with our strategic objectives while maintaining overall financial stability."

By incorporating ChatGPT into your decision-making process, you gain access to its vast knowledge base and analytical capabilities that may not be readily available within your organization alone.

Moreover, when it comes to tax planning strategies or optimizing profitability by reducing costs or increasing revenue streams; ChatG-PT can provide valuable guidance based on historical data analysis and expert knowledge in the field.

Of course, human judgment remains essential in decision-making processes. However, by augmenting your own expertise with the power of ChatGPT, you can make more informed decisions and increase your chances of success.

Now let's examine another example:

CEO: "ChatGPT, what would be the impact of increasing our marketing budget by 20%?"

ChatGPT: "By increasing the marketing budget by 20%, we can expect a potential increase in customer acquisition and brand awareness. However, it's important to consider market saturation, competition, and customer behavior analysis before making a final decision."

The dialogue above demonstrates how ChatGPT can assist in strategic planning discussions at the highest levels of an organization. It provides valuable insights that help leaders weigh different options and make well- informed decisions.

However, as with any tool or technology, there are always ethical considerations to keep in mind. In Chapter 6, we will delve deeper into these concerns and discuss strategies for responsible AI usage. Integrating ChatGPT into strategic planning and decision-making processes can significantly enhance productivity and improve outcomes. By leveraging its analytical capabilities and vast knowledge base, you can make well-informed decisions quickly while considering various factors that impact your business success.

Remember that human judgment remains essential. ChatGPT is a tool to augment your decision-making process rather than replace it entirely. In the next chapter, we will explore how to streamline business correspondence using ChatGPT as your virtual writing partner. Embrace the power of ChatGPT to master strategic planning and decision making for success in today's dynamic business world!

Chapter 4: Business Correspondence and Communication with Chatgpt

Making ChatGPT a Business Partner

In the realm of business, the integration of artificial intelligence (AI) has become a game-changer. ChatGPT, with its advanced natural language processing capabilities, stands out as an exceptional AI tool that can be leveraged as a business partner. Unlike traditional software tools, ChatGPT offers a conversational interface that can adapt to various business needs, from customer service to decision support systems.

One of the most significant advantages of making ChatGPT a business partner is its ability to handle repetitive and time-consuming tasks. For instance, it can manage customer inquiries through chatbots, providing instant responses and freeing up human employees for more complex issues. This not only improves efficiency but also enhances customer satisfaction by reducing wait times. Moreover, ChatGPT can be trained on company-specific data to provide personalized assistance. Imagine an AI assistant that knows your product catalog inside out and can make recommendations based on customer preferences or past purchases. This level of personalization was once the domain of experienced sales associates but can now be replicated at scale with AI.

Chapter 5: Research and Education through ChatGPT

Role of ChatGPT in Research

The integration of ChatGPT into the research process marks a significant shift in how information is synthesized, ideas are generated, and data is analyzed. Researchers across various disciplines are finding that ChatGPT can serve as an invaluable tool for enhancing their work, from the initial brainstorming phase to the final stages of publication.

One of the primary roles ChatGPT plays in research is as an idea generator. When researchers approach a new topic or hit a creative block, interacting with ChatGPT can provide a fresh perspective or suggest novel angles to explore. For instance, when examining the impact of climate change on urban planning, ChatGPT might propose considering socio- economic factors or historical precedents that could enrich the study.

Moreover, ChatGPT's ability to process and summarize large volumes of literature quickly makes it an excellent assistant for conducting comprehensive literature reviews. Researchers can input abstracts or summaries and receive synthesized overviews that highlight key themes and findings. This not only saves time but also ensures that no critical piece of literature is overlooked.

Data analysis is another area where ChatGPT shows promise. In fields like social sciences or humanities where qualitative data analysis is prevalent, researchers can use ChatGPT to identify patterns within textual data sets. For example, when analyzing interview transcripts for a study on migration narratives, researchers could employ ChatGPT to detect recurring motifs or sentiments expressed by participants.

However, while leveraging this AI technology in research offers numerous advantages, it also necessitates a critical approach. Researchers must verify the accuracy of information provided by ChatGPT and ensure it aligns with validated sources. Additionally, ethical considerations around authorship and intellectual property arise when using AI-generated content; thus, clear guidelines must be established regarding its use in academic publications.

Teaching and Education through ChatGPT

ChatGPT's role in education extends beyond being just another digital tool; it has become an interactive platform that fosters learning through engagement and personalization. Educators are harnessing its capabilities to create dynamic learning environments where students can explore subjects deeply and at their own pace.

In classroom settings, teachers utilize ChatGPT to design interactive activities that cater to different learning styles. For instance, visual learners might benefit from AI-generated infographics explaining complex scientific processes while kinesthetic learners could engage with simulations prompted by questions posed to the AI.

Furthermore, language educators find great value in using ChatGPT for practicing conversational skills with students. By simulating natural dialogues in various languages and contexts—ranging from casual street conversations to formal interviews—students gain confidence and fluency without feeling self-conscious about making mistakes with human partners.

ChatGPT also serves as an on-demand tutor providing explanations tailored to individual student queries outside class hours. Whether it's solving math problems step-by-step or offering insights into Shakespearean plays' thematic elements, students have access to personalized assistance anytime they need it.

Despite these benefits, educators must navigate potential pitfalls such as ensuring academic integrity (preventing plagiarism) and fostering critical thinking rather than reliance on AI-generated answers. Moreover, privacy concerns regarding student interactions with AI platforms need addressing through strict data protection policies.

Training Programs Enhanced by ChatGPT

Incorporating ChatGPT into training programs has revolutionized how professional development is approached across industries. The adaptability of this technology allows for customized training experiences that cater not only to industry-specific knowledge but also soft skills enhancement. For example, customer service representatives undergo training modules facilitated by ChatGPT where they encounter various customer scenarios requiring empathy and problem-solving skills. Through these simulated interactions powered by natural language processing capabilities of AI like GTP-3 (which powers OpenAI's chatbots), trainees learn effective communication strategies applicable in real-life situations without risking customer dissatisfaction during their learning curve.

Similarly, leadership training programs leverage chatbot simulations for conflict resolution exercises wherein emerging leaders practice navigating difficult conversations—a crucial skill set for any managerial role—by engaging with realistic virtual counterparts programmed with diverse personality types and responses.

In healthcare settings too, medical professionals benefit from continuous education facilitated by tools like GTP-3 which keep them updated on latest practices through digestible content formats such as Q&A sessions or scenario-based learning exercises designed around patient care protocols or new treatment methodologies. While these advancements offer promising avenues for enhanced learning experiences within training programs across sectors—from corporate environments to healthcare facilities—it remains imperative that trainers maintain oversight over content quality assurance ensuring alignment with up-to-date standards within respective fields alongside monitoring participant engagement levels throughout program durations ensuring optimal outcomes from investments made into integrating such innovative technologies into professional development initiatives globally.

Chapter 6: Personalized Learning Experience with ChatGPT

Language Skills Development using ChatGPT

The advent of AI language models like ChatGPT has revolutionized the way we approach language learning. By providing an interactive platform, learners can engage in real-time conversations, receive instant feedback, and practice their writing skills in a variety of contexts. This immersive experience is akin to having a personal tutor available 24/7, catering to the learner's pace and style.

One of the most significant advantages of using ChatGPT for language development is its ability to simulate natural conversations.

Learners can converse on a multitude of topics, ranging from everyday small talk to discussing complex subject matter. This not only helps in building vocabulary but also aids in understanding the nuances of language such as idioms, colloquialisms, and cultural references.

Moreover, writing exercises with ChatGPT can be highly beneficial for learners. They can write essays, reports, or creative stories and receive immediate feedback on grammar, syntax, and style. Unlike traditional methods that may take days for feedback to be returned, ChatGPT's instantaneous responses allow for rapid learning cycles.

Incorporating storytelling into language learning is another area where ChatGPT shines. Learners can create narratives with the AI's assistance, which helps them think critically about plot development and character creation while practicing their language skills. This method not only makes learning more enjoyable but also more memorable due to the emotional connection often formed through storytelling.

However, it's important to note that while ChatGPT provides an excellent avenue for practice and reinforcement of language skills learned elsewhere, it should complement formal education rather than replace it entirely. The guidance of a human educator is invaluable for addressing complex questions or correcting persistent errors that an AI might not catch.

Explaining Complex Concepts via ChatGPT

ChatGPT serves as an exceptional tool when it comes to breaking down complex concepts into digestible explanations. Its capacity to process vast amounts of information allows it to provide comprehensive overviews on intricate subjects across various fields such as science, technology, engineering, mathematics (STEM), humanities, and social sciences.

For instance, when dealing with abstract mathematical theories or principles in physics that are difficult for students to visualize or comprehend through traditional textbooks alone, ChatGPT can offer alternative explanations or analogies that make these concepts more relatable. It could compare the concept of gravitational pull to the feeling one experiences when being drawn toward the ground on a swing set—making abstract scientific ideas tangible through everyday experiences. Furthermore, educators can leverage ChatGPT's capabilities by integrating it into lesson plans where students interact with the AI model after classroom instruction. Students could pose questions about parts they find confusing and receive clarifications tailored specifically to their level of understanding—a form of differentiated instruction that would be challenging for teachers to provide individually at scale.

It's also worth noting that explaining complex concepts isn't solely about simplifying information; it's about engaging learners' critical thinking skills by presenting multiple perspectives or applications of a theory. For example, when discussing economic models like supply and demand curves with business students, ChatGPT could illustrate how these models apply differently in various real-world scenarios such as technology markets versus agricultural markets.

Answering Learners' Queries through ChatGPT

ChatGPT stands out as an educational resource due to its ability to answer learners' queries promptly and accurately. This feature is particularly useful because it caters directly to individual learner curiosities and knowledge gaps—something that is often logistically challenging within classroom settings due to time constraints and teacher-to-student ratios.

When learners approach ChatGPT with questions ranging from simple factual inquiries ("What is photosynthesis?") to more profound philosophical ponderings ("What are the ethical implications of artificial intelligence?"), they receive tailored responses that encourage further exploration rather than just rote answers.

Additionally, this personalized interaction fosters a sense of autonomy among learners; they are empowered to direct their own education journey by seeking answers at their own pace without fear of judgment—a factor especially crucial for adult education or shy individuals who may hesitate to ask questions in public forums. However impressive this feature may be though; educators must emphasize critical evaluation skills alongside using AI tools like ChatGPT. While AI responses are generally reliable within certain contexts (like known scientific facts), they may falter when dealing with subjective analysis or emerging research areas where consensus has yet been established within academic communities.

In conclusion:

- Language Skills Development: Using chatbots like GPT enhances conversational abilities and written communication through interactive engagement.

- Explaining Complex Concepts: These tools serve as digital teaching assistants providing alternative explanations which aid comprehension.

- Answering Learners' Queries: They offer personalized support answering diverse questions but should be used alongside critical thinking exercises ensuring understanding beyond surface-level responses. Each application underscores how AI technologies like chatbots have become integral components within modern educational ecosystems—augmenting traditional teaching methodologies while fostering innovative learning experiences tailored towards individual needs.

Chapter 7: Ethical Considerations in Educational Use of ChatGPT

Responsible Use of AI Models in Education

The integration of AI models like ChatGPT into educational settings has the potential to revolutionize how students learn and teachers instruct. However, this integration must be approached with a sense of responsibility to ensure that the technology is used to enhance, rather than detract from, the educational experience. Responsible use involves understanding the capabilities and limitations of AI, setting clear boundaries for its application, and ensuring that it supports pedagogical goals.

One aspect of responsible use is maintaining academic integrity. While ChatGPT can assist students in learning and completing assignments, educators must establish guidelines to prevent plagiarism and encourage original thought. For instance, teachers could design tasks that require critical thinking and personal reflection, which are difficult for AI to replicate. Additionally, they might use AI as a tool for drafting or brainstorming while emphasizing the importance of students' own contributions to their work.

Another consideration is the role of teachers in an AI-enhanced classroom. Rather than replacing educators, ChatGPT should serve as an aid that complements their expertise. Teachers can leverage AI for administrative tasks such as grading or providing initial feedback on assignments, freeing up time to focus on personalized instruction and student engagement. Furthermore, educators should be trained not only in how to use AI tools effectively but also in recognizing when human intervention is necessary. For example, if a student relies too heavily on ChatGPT for problem-solving without understanding the underlying concepts, a teacher's guidance becomes crucial.

Incorporating real-world examples into lessons using ChatGPT can also foster responsible use by connecting abstract concepts to practical applications. This approach helps students see the relevance of their studies and encourages them to think critically about how they apply knowledge outside the classroom.

Addressing Biases and Misinformation in AI Education

AI systems like ChatGPT are only as unbiased as the data they are trained on. Since these models often learn from vast datasets culled from the internet—which includes biased and incorrect information—they can inadvertently perpetuate these issues. Addressing biases and misinformation requires proactive measures from both developers and educators.

Developers have a responsibility to continually refine AI models to reduce biases. This involves curating training datasets more carefully and developing algorithms that can identify and correct biased patterns in data processing. OpenAI has made strides in this area by implementing moderation tools designed to flag potentially biased content generated by ChatGPT.

Educators play a critical role by teaching students how to critically evaluate information provided by AI systems. They can introduce exercises that challenge students to identify potential biases within generated content or compare AI-generated explanations with authoritative sources.

Case studies highlighting instances where reliance on biased AI led to real-world consequences can serve as powerful teaching tools about the importance of critical evaluation skills. For example, discussing how biased algorithms have affected credit scoring or job recruitment processes illustrates tangible impacts of unchecked biases. Moreover, incorporating discussions about ethical data sourcing into curricula raises awareness among future technologists about their role in preventing bias at its source—during dataset creation and model training phases.

Privacy and Data Security Implications

The deployment of ChatGPT within educational institutions necessitates stringent attention to privacy concerns and data security protocols due to sensitive nature of student data involved. Privacy considerations include ensuring that any personal information shared with or generated by ChatGPT remains confidential according to laws like FERPA (Family

Educational Rights and Privacy Act) in the United States or GDPR (General Data Protection Regulation) in Europe. Data security involves protecting against unauthorized access or leaks of student information through robust cybersecurity measures such as encryption during data transmission between users' devices and servers hosting ChatGPT services.

Educational institutions must establish clear policies regarding who has access rights over data generated through interactions with ChatGPT— whether it's homework assignments or casual conversations—and under what circumstances this data may be analyzed or shared further. Anecdotes from schools experiencing breaches due either lax security practices around third-party educational apps illustrate just how damaging neglecting these aspects can be—not only legally but also trust-wise between schools families involved.

To mitigate risks associated with privacy data security implications when using chatbots like ChatGPT education sector stakeholders need collaborate closely: developers must prioritize building secure platforms; administrators need enforce strict compliance standards; teachers should educate themselves their pupils about safe digital practices; parents guardians ought remain vigilant regarding children's online activities especially those related schoolwork involving external software tools.

Inclusivity should be at the forefront when utilizing ChatGPT for various purposes. Ensuring that individuals from diverse backgrounds have equal access to AI technologies is paramount for building an inclusive future. Developers should actively strive to train models on diverse datasets and implement safeguards against discriminatory behavior.

AI systems like ChatGPT should never be used to propagate hate speech, misinformation, or harmful content. Responsible use of AI entails employing it for positive and constructive purposes, while actively discouraging and preventing its misuse. By adhering to ethical guidelines and fostering a culture of responsible AI usage, we can harness the full potential of ChatGPT for societal benefit.

As we navigate the ethical considerations surrounding AI usage, it is important to remember that technology alone cannot solve all our problems. Human judgment and empathy are irreplaceable components in decision- making processes. ChatGPT should be seen as a tool that complements human intelligence rather than replacing it.

Chapter 8: Utilizing ChatGPT in Research

Idea Generation with ChatGPT

The process of generating ideas is fundamental to the advancement of research and development across all disciplines. ChatGPT, as an AI language model, offers a unique platform for brainstorming and ideation that can significantly enhance this creative process. By leveraging its vast database of knowledge and linguistic patterns, researchers can use ChatGPT to break through cognitive barriers and explore new territories of thought.

One of the most significant advantages of using ChatGPT for idea generation is its ability to provide immediate feedback on concepts. Researchers can input their initial thoughts and receive instant suggestions on how to expand or refine them. This iterative dialogue with an AI can lead to the discovery of angles and perspectives that might not have been immediately apparent. For instance, in the field of environmental science, a researcher exploring sustainable energy solutions could use ChatGPT to generate ideas on novel materials for solar cells or innovative urban planning strategies that integrate renewable energy sources.

Moreover, ChatGPT's capacity to draw from diverse fields can foster interdisciplinary approaches to problem-solving. A medical researcher working on a new drug delivery system might find inspiration from advancements in nanotechnology or materials science suggested by the AI, leading to breakthroughs that would have been less likely within the siloed confines of a single discipline.

However, it's crucial for researchers to remain critical and discerning when sifting through AI-generated ideas. Not all suggestions will be practical or relevant; thus, human expertise is essential in evaluating the feasibility and potential impact of each idea. Additionally, while ChatGPT can simulate creativity up to a point, it cannot replace the intuitive leaps and associative thinking inherent in human creativity—qualities that often lead to groundbreaking innovations.

Exploring Different Perspectives using ChatGPT

Research thrives on the examination and synthesis of multiple viewpoints. In this regard, ChatGPT serves as an invaluable tool for exploring different perspectives on any given topic. Its programming allows it to simulate various stances or theoretical frameworks without bias—a feature particularly useful when tackling controversial or multifaceted issues.

For example, consider a political scientist researching governance models. By engaging with ChatGPT, they could explore arguments for and against different systems such as democracy, authoritarianism, socialism, or libertarianism. The AI could present historical examples, theoretical justifications, critiques from various scholars—all without personal bias affecting the output.

This capability extends beyond academic debate; it also has practical applications in policy analysis where understanding diverse viewpoints is crucial for crafting inclusive policies. A policy analyst could use ChatGPT to anticipate objections from stakeholders by examining potential impacts through different lenses—economic efficiency versus social equity being one common dichotomy.

It's important for users engaging with these perspectives via ChatGPT not only to absorb information but also critically engage with it—questioning assumptions made by the AI and seeking out empirical evidence where necessary. While ChatGPT may offer a starting point for understanding different views, it cannot fully replicate the depth of knowledge held by experts who have dedicated years studying their respective fields.

Data Analysis and Literature Reviews with ChatGPT

In research endeavors where data analysis plays a central role—be it qualitative or quantitative—ChatGPT can act as an assistant capable of handling large volumes of information efficiently. Researchers inundated with data sets can employ this tool in preliminary analyses: summarizing trends, identifying outliers or anomalies, or even suggesting possible correlations between variables.

When conducting literature reviews—a task known both for its importance and laborious nature—ChatGPT's ability to quickly digest vast amounts of text becomes invaluable. It can help researchers stay abreast of recent publications by providing summaries or highlighting key themes across numerous studies within minutes—a task that would otherwise take hours if done manually.

Furthermore, integrating natural language processing capabilities allows researchers using ChatGPT not just passive summaries but also active engagement with content through question-answering formats about specific details within papers reviewed—an interactive approach that may reveal insights which static reading might miss.

Yet reliance on AI must be tempered with caution; literature reviews are nuanced undertakings requiring critical appraisal skills beyond mere summarization abilities possessed by current AI technologies like GPT models. Researchers should verify findings suggested by GTP against original sources ensuring accuracy before drawing conclusions based upon them.

In conclusion, across these three areas—Idea Generation Exploring Different Perspectives, Data Analysis and Literature Reviews—ChatGPt stands out as powerful adjunctive tool enhancing productivity creativity within research processes while simultaneously demanding careful oversight ensure integrity scholarly work remains uncompromised presence artificial intelligence assistance.

Chapter 9: Critical Evaluation of Content Generated by ChatGPT

Verifying Accuracy of Generated Content

In the realm of AI-generated content, verifying accuracy is paramount. ChatGPT, like any other language model, synthesizes information based on patterns learned from a vast corpus of data. However, this does not guarantee the veracity of its outputs. To ensure reliability, several strategies must be employed.

Firstly, cross-referencing is essential. Users should compare the information provided by ChatGPT with reputable sources. For instance, if ChatGPT offers statistical data or historical facts, these should be checkedagainst academic databases or official records. In cases where ChatGPT is used for research purposes, it's crucial to corroborate findings with peer- reviewed articles and empirical evidence.

Another aspect involves understanding the model's training data limitations. Since ChatGPT's knowledge is capped at a certain point in time (the knowledge cutoff), any events or developments occurring after that date are unknown to it. Users must stay abreast of recent advancements and updates in their field to fill in these gaps.

Moreover, users can employ a technique known as triangulation—using multiple methods or sources to validate the generated content. For example, when using ChatGPT for strategic planning or budgeting advice, one could combine its suggestions with industry benchmarks and insights from financial experts to ensure robustness.

Real-world examples highlight the importance of accuracy verification. Consider a business using ChatGPT for market analysis; an inaccurate trend prediction could lead to misguided strategies and financial loss. Therefore, businesses often use AI-generated insights as a starting point rather than a definitive solution.

Lastly, feedback loops can enhance accuracy over time. By reporting inaccuracies back to developers or through user interfaces designed for this purpose, models like ChatGPT can be fine-tuned to produce more reliable outputs.

Role of Human Expertise and Judgment

Human expertise and judgment are irreplaceable components in the utilization of AI tools such as ChatGPT. While AI can process information at unprecedented speeds and volumes, it lacks the nuanced understanding and ethical reasoning that humans possess. The role of human expertise becomes evident when dealing with complex problems that require contextual interpretation—a task at which humans excel but AI often falters. For instance, in legal advice or taxation matters where nuances and subtleties play significant roles, professionals rely on their deep domain knowledge to interpret AI suggestions appropriately.

Human judgment also plays a critical role in ethical considerations. When using ChatGPT for education or communication purposes, educators and communicators must ensure that the content aligns with societal norms and values—a responsibility that cannot be fully entrusted to an algorithmic model. Furthermore, human intuition is vital when evaluating AI-generated content's plausibility. A seasoned researcher might notice subtle inconsistencies in literature reviews conducted by ChatGPT that would otherwise go undetected by less experienced individuals.

Case studies have shown how human-AI collaboration can yield superior results compared to either working alone. In medical diagnostics, for example, combining AI's pattern recognition capabilities with doctors' clinical experience enhances diagnostic accuracy while reducing time spent on routine image analysis tasks.

Limitations of AI-generated Content

Despite its impressive capabilities, AI-generated content has inherent limitations that users must navigate carefully. One significant limitation is context comprehension—AI may struggle with understanding nuanced human interactions or cultural references that are second nature to people.

For instance, when generating social media posts or scripts for branding purposes using ChatGPT, marketers must review content thoroughly to ensure it resonates with their target audience's cultural context and brand voice—something an AI might misinterpret due to lack of real-world experience.

Additionally, while models like ChatGPT can simulate creativity up to a point by remixing existing ideas in novel ways—they do not truly innovate in the way humans do. Authors using ChatGPT for writing books still need their creative spark to breathe life into stories beyond what an algorithm can generate based on existing literature patterns. AI also faces challenges with tasks requiring detailed explanations or advanced problem-solving skills—areas where deep expertise is necessary—for example coding complex software systems or developing intricate business strategies where multiple variables interact dynamically over time.

Moreover, there are concerns about perpetuating biases present within training data sets—a serious issue given how biases can affect decision- making processes across various sectors including recruitment practices or loan approvals where fairness is critical. In conclusionary remarks regarding these limitations—it's clear that while tools like ChatGPT offer substantial benefits across diverse applications—their effective use hinges upon recognizing their constraints alongside leveraging human oversight for quality control ensuring ethical standards are upheld throughout all stages of interaction between humans and artificial intelligence systems alike.

Chapter 10: Legal Advice through ChatGPT

Drafting Legal Documents with ChatGPT

The advent of AI technologies like ChatGPT has revolutionized the way legal documents are drafted. Lawyers and legal professionals now have access to a tool that can assist in creating complex legal documents with greater efficiency. ChatGPT, with its advanced language processing capabilities, can generate drafts of contracts, agreements, wills, and other legal paperwork that form the backbone of legal practice.

When drafting legal documents with ChatGPT, one begins by providing the AI with specific information about the document's purpose and the parties involved. For instance, when drafting a lease agreement, one would input details regarding the property, lease term, payment conditions, and any clauses specific to the situation at hand.

ChatGPT can then use thisinformation to produce a tailored draft that reflects these requirements.

However, it is not just about generating text; it's also about ensuring that the language used is legally sound and precise. Legal drafting requires not only correct terminology but also clarity and enforceability. Herein lies an advantage of using AI: it can draw from a vast database of legal phrases and clauses to ensure that documents meet these criteria.

Moreover, for routine or standardized documents such as non-disclosure agreements or terms of service for websites, ChatGPT can significantly speed up the process. By automating parts of these tasks, law firms can reduce turnaround times for their clients while maintaining high standards of accuracy.

Real-world examples include small businesses utilizing AI-generated templates for their contracts or startups employing chatbots to draft initial versions of privacy policies. These tools allow entrepreneurs to focus on their business rather than getting bogged down by initial legal formalities. Nevertheless, while AI can provide a strong starting point for document creation, human oversight remains crucial. Lawyers must review and customize AI-generated drafts to ensure they fully address all nuances and unique aspects of each case.

Initial Guidance on Legal Matters through ChatGPT

ChatGPT serves as an accessible first point of contact for individuals seeking guidance on various legal matters. Whether someone is dealing with a landlord-tenant dispute or seeking advice on intellectual property rights, initial interactions with an AI like ChatGPT can help clarify options before consulting a lawyer.

For example, if someone believes they have been wrongfully terminated from their job, they might turn to ChatGPT for an understanding of their rights under employment law. The AI could provide general information about wrongful termination cases and what constitutes unfair dismissal according to jurisdiction-specific laws.

This preliminary guidance is particularly valuable in areas where there may be confusion due to overlapping regulations or complex statutory language. By breaking down information into more digestible pieces, individuals gain better insight into their situations without feeling overwhelmed by legalese.

Furthermore, in scenarios where individuals are unsure whether they require professional legal assistance or not—such as understanding copyright laws when publishing online content—ChatGPT can offer explanations that help them make informed decisions about seeking further help.

In educational settings too—law schools or paralegal training programs— ChatGPT could be used as a teaching aid where students interact with the AI to test their knowledge on hypothetical cases or explore different facets of law through guided questioning by the bot. However important this initial guidance may be though; it cannot replace personalized advice from qualified attorneys who understand the full context surrounding a client's issue. Initial guidance should always be followed up by expert consultation where necessary.

Limitations of AI in Legal Advice

While artificial intelligence offers promising applications within the field of law, its limitations must be acknowledged especially when it comes to providing reliable legal advice. One significant limitation stems from an inherent characteristic: AI systems like ChatGPT lack human judgment which is often critical in nuanced legal analysis.

Legal advice frequently involves interpreting laws that may be open- ended or subjectively applied depending on circumstances—a task requiring human discernment which current AIs are unable to replicate fully. For instance, predicting how a judge might rule based on precedent involves subtleties beyond mere data analysis; it requires understanding judicial discretion and interpretive tendencies which are deeply rooted in human experience and intuition.

Additionally, while AIs operate based on patterns found within large datasets including past cases and statutes; they do not possess consciousness nor moral reasoning capabilities essential for ethical considerations within law practice such as conflicts-of-interest assessments or determining equitable outcomes beyond what's written in black-and-white text.

Another limitation concerns data privacy issues associated with using cloud-based AI services like ChatGPT for sensitive matters involving confidential client information—a concern paramount within attorney-client privilege obligations. Moreover; since AIs rely heavily on existing data sources; there's potential risk related misinformation if those sources contain errors or biases which could inadvertently perpetuate injustices particularly against marginalized groups already facing systemic discrimination within judicial systems worldwide.

Lastly; given rapid changes occurring across many areas (e.g., technology laws); AIs may struggle keeping pace unless continuously updated—an aspect requiring vigilance from users relying upon them. In conclusion; while leveraging tools such as ChatGPT presents opportunities enhancing productivity within certain aspects (like document drafting); caution must prevail ensuring ethical standards remain uncompromised alongside recognition towards inherent limitations currently faced by artificial intelligence offering "legal advice".

Chapter 11: Getting Started with ChatGPT

Familiarizing with Capabilities and Limitations of ChatGPT

ChatGPT, a variant of the GPT (Generative Pretrained Transformer) model developed by OpenAI, has been making waves across various industries due to its advanced natural language processing capabilities. It can engage in human-like conversations, answer questions, and generate text that is often indistinguishable from that written by humans. This has opened up a plethora of applications ranging from customer service automation to aiding in creative writing.

One of the most remarkable capabilities of ChatGPT is its ability to understand and generate text in multiple languages, making it an invaluable tool for global communication. Its proficiency in language tasks allows it to perform translation services, summarize articles, and even create content for social media platforms. In the educational sector, ChatGPT serves as a virtual tutor providing explanations for complex subjects and offering practice exercises tailored to students' learning needs.

However, despite these impressive abilities, ChatGPT is not without limitations. One significant drawback is its occasional generation of incorrect or nonsensical responses. The model's understanding is based on patterns within the data it was trained on rather than actual comprehension of facts or concepts. This means that while it can simulate conversation about quantum physics or international law, it does not "understand" these topics in the way a human expert would.

Another limitation lies in context awareness. While ChatGPT can maintain context over a conversation thread reasonably well, it may struggle with more nuanced contexts or when required to integrate complex cross-topic knowledge seamlessly. Additionally, there are concerns about its tendency to produce biased outputs since machine learning models can inadvertently learn biases present in their training data.

In terms of creativity, authors have found ChatGPT useful for overcoming writer's block by generating ideas or dialogue snippets. However, relying too heavily on AI-generated content risks diluting the unique voice and creativity that define an author's work. It should be seen as an assistant rather than a replacement for human ingenuity.

Understanding these capabilities and limitations is crucial for anyone looking to integrate ChatGPT into their workflow effectively. By leveraging its strengths and compensating for its weaknesses through careful oversight and fact-checking, users can harness this powerful tool without falling prey to its pitfalls.

Understanding the Training Process of AI Models

The training process behind AI models like ChatGPT is both intricate and fascinating. At its core lies machine learning—a subset of artificial intelligence where algorithms improve through experience without being explicitly programmed for each task they perform. To train such models, researchers use vast datasets comprising text from books, websites, articles—essentially any source that provides diverse linguistic patterns and structures. The model learns by predicting the next word in a sentence given all previous words (a task known as unsupervised learning). Through repeated exposure to different ways language is used across millions of documents, the model begins to grasp grammar rules, idiomatic expressions, factual information about the world, stylistic nuances among genres—and much more.

This process requires substantial computational resources; training state- of-the-art models like GPT-3 involves weeks or months on clusters of high- end GPUs or TPUs (Tensor Processing Units). The result is a neural network with billions—or even trillions—of parameters fine-tuned during this extensive training phase. However sophisticated this process may be though; it's not infallible. For instance: if certain viewpoints are overrepresented in training data while others are underrepresented or absent altogether—the resulting model will likely exhibit biases reflecting those imbalances. To mitigate such issues requires careful curation of training datasets along with techniques like differential privacy which help ensure individual data points don't unduly influence outcomes.

Moreover: because AI models learn correlations rather than causations— they might associate words together based on frequency rather than meaning leading them astray when dealing with less common topics or emerging trends they haven't encountered before. Understanding these intricacies helps users appreciate why even advanced

AI like ChatGPT sometimes makes mistakes—and emphasizes why ongoing research into areas like transfer learning (where knowledge gained from one task helps perform another) remains critical for future advancements.

Exercising Caution while Using AI Models

As we embrace the power of AI tools like ChatGPT across various domains—from drafting legal contracts to crafting marketing strategies—it's imperative we exercise caution ensuring responsible usage aligns with ethical standards while safeguarding against potential harms.

Firstly: transparency around how AI-generated content is used becomes essential especially when such content could influence opinions or decisions—as seen with news articles social media posts academic papers etcetera... Users must disclose involvement artificial intelligence creation process avoid misleading readers into believing solely human-produced work involved which could erode trust once discovered otherwise...

Secondly: vigilance against perpetuating existing biases cannot be overstated... Since machine-learning algorithms reflect biases present within their training data—there exists risk reinforcing stereotypes spreading misinformation unless proactive measures taken counteract such tendencies... This includes implementing fairness-aware algorithms conducting regular audits outputs ensure diversity inclusiveness respected throughout...

Furthermore: privacy considerations must front center when deploying conversational AIs... Personal information shared during interactions potentially sensitive nature thus robust protocols need place protect user data unauthorized access misuse... Companies institutions adopting technology should adhere strictest standards compliance regulations like GDPR CCPA...

Lastly: reliance solely upon automated systems decision-making poses risks particularly areas requiring nuanced judgment empathy—for example healthcare legal advice mental health support... While AIs provide assistance streamline processes ultimate responsibility lies humans oversee verify accuracy appropriateness advice given ensuring compassionate understanding remains forefront interactio ns...

In conclusion navigating complexities associated using advanced technologies such as ChatGPT demands thoughtful approach balancing innovation ethical considerations... By staying informed current developments maintaining critical perspective towards outputs generated— we better positioned exploit benefits whilst minimizing downsides associated burgeoning field artificial intelligence...

Chapter 12: Writing Books with ChatGPT

Idea Generation for Authors using ChatGPT

The process of writing a book often begins with the spark of an idea. For authors, finding that initial inspiration can sometimes be the most challenging part of the creative journey. This is where ChatGPT can become an invaluable asset in the ideation phase. By leveraging its vast database and language processing capabilities, ChatGPT can help authors overcome writer's block and generate a plethora of ideas for stories, themes, settings, and even genres they might not have considered.

Authors can engage with ChatGPT by posing questions or presenting scenarios to see how the AI responds with suggestions. For instance, if an author is interested in writing a science fiction novel but isn't sure about the specifics, they could ask ChatGPT to list potential futuristic technologies that could influence society. The AI might come back with ideas ranging from artificial intelligence governance to interstellar travel implications.

Moreover, ChatGPT can assist in expanding upon a seedling idea. An author might have a basic concept such as "a world where dreams can be recorded and replayed." By interacting with ChatGPT, they could explore various subplots, ethical dilemmas, character conflicts, and societal changes that such a technology could entail.

Another way authors can use ChatGPT is by feeding it snippets of information or data relevant to their desired topic. The AI can then synthesize this information into unique perspectives or story angles that may not be immediately obvious to human cognition due to inherent biases or cognitive patterns.

However, while generating ideas with ChatGPT can open up new avenues for creativity, it's essential for authors to remember that these suggestions are starting points. It remains their responsibility to flesh out these ideas into compelling narratives that reflect their voice and vision.

Character Development using ChatGPT

Creating memorable characters is at the heart of storytelling. Characters drive the plot forward and connect readers emotionally to the narrative. With ChatGPT's assistance, authors can delve deeper into character development by exploring personalities, backstories, motivations, and dynamics in ways they might not have initially envisioned.

ChatGPT serves as an interactive sounding board for character creation. Authors can "interview" their characters through the AI by typing out questions they believe their characters would face within their story's context. This exercise helps in understanding how characters would react under different circumstances—thereby adding layers of depth and realism. Furthermore, writers can use ChatGPT to experiment with dialogue styles and voices for each character. By inputting specific traits or accents into the chatbot and asking it to generate dialogue samples, authors gain insights into how their characters might speak or interact with others within their world.

An additional benefit comes from using ChatGPT to simulate interactions between characters before they are written into scenes. This pre-writing strategy allows authors to identify potential chemistry or conflict between characters which could lead to more dynamic scenes when actually penned down. It's also worth noting that because AI doesn't possess human emotions but has been trained on emotional language patterns; it offers unique perspectives on emotional responses which may challenge an author's conventional approach towards character emotionality—potentially leading them toward more nuanced portrayals.

Co-writing Sections of a Book with ChatGPT

The act of co-writing traditionally involves two (or more) writers collaborating on a piece of work—each contributing their own expertise and style. Involving ChatGPT in this process introduces an unconventional partner whose strengths lie in its ability to quickly generate text based on given prompts or guidelines set forth by its human counterpart(s). When co-writing sections of a book with ChatGPT, authors should first establish clear objectives for what they want from each section—whether it's developing exposition-heavy passages or crafting intricate plot developments—and communicate these goals effectively through prompts given to the AI.

One practical application is utilizing ChatGPT for drafting difficult-to-write sections like technical explanations within non-fiction works or elaborate fantasy world-building elements where consistency in detail is key but often laborious for humans alone. In fiction writing specifically; if an author struggles with certain types of scenes (e.g., action sequences), they could outline what needs happening in those scenes and let ChatGPT fill in the blanks—providing a rough draft which then gets refined through human touch ensuring stylistic coherence throughout the book.

Additionally, since revision is integral part writing process; after initial drafts are completed (either by human alone or alongside AI), authors return these drafts back into conversation with chatbot seeking alternative phrasings or structural improvements thus engaging iterative feedback loop enhancing overall quality output before finalizing manuscript ready publication.

In conclusion; whether sparking initial concepts during brainstorming sessions deepening complexities fictional personas co-authoring segments literature; incorporating intelligent tools like presents exciting opportunities augment traditional methods employed writers across globe however always bearing mind ultimate creative control rests firmly hands individuals wielding tool rather than tool itself ensuring authenticity originality preserved every step way.

Chapter 13: Ethical Considerations in Using ChatGPT

Responsible Use of AI Models

The responsible use of AI models like ChatGPT extends beyond mere functional applications; it encompasses a commitment to ethical principles that guide the deployment and interaction with these technologies. As AI systems become more integrated into various sectors, including education, research, and legal advice, the imperative for responsible usage becomes paramount.

One aspect of responsible use is ensuring that AI models are employed as tools to augment human capabilities rather than replace them. In educational settings, while ChatGPT can offer personalized feedback and aid in language practice or concept explanation, it should not supplant the role of educators who provide nuanced understanding and mentorship.

Similarly, in research, ChatGPT's ability to analyze data or conduct literature reviews must be complemented by critical human analysis to validate findings and maintain scientific rigor. Moreover, deploying AI responsibly entails continuous monitoring for unintended consequences. For instance, when used in strategic planning or budgeting within businesses, reliance on AI-generated insights must be balanced with expert oversight to prevent potential missteps due to algorithmic limitations or data inaccuracies.

Another dimension of responsibility is transparency about the capabilities and limitations of AI models. Users should be informed about what ChatGPT can do reliably—such as generating ideas or assisting with coding—and where its suggestions need verification—like in legal document drafting or taxation matters. Furthermore, developers and users alike must engage in ongoing dialogue about the ethical implications of AI advancements. This includes discussions around the potential displacement of jobs by automation and how society might adapt to such changes.

Real-world examples underscore the importance of responsible use. For instance, when Microsoft's chatbot Tay was released on Twitter without sufficient safeguards, it quickly learned harmful language from interactions with users. This incident highlights the necessity for robust safety measures and ethical considerations before deployment.

In conclusion, responsible use of AI models demands a holistic approach that considers not only their technical capabilities but also their broader impact on society. It requires collaboration between developers, users, ethicists, and policymakers to ensure these powerful tools serve humanity's best interests without causing inadvertent harm.

Addressing Harmful or Biased Content

The proliferation of AI-generated content has brought forth concerns regarding harmful or biased outputs that may perpetuate stereotypes or spread misinformation. Addressing these issues is crucial for maintaining trust in AI technologies like ChatGPT. Bias can seep into AI models through skewed training datasets that reflect historical prejudices or societal inequalities. To combat this issue proactively, developers must employ diverse datasets that represent a wide range of perspectives. Additionally, implementing algorithms designed to detect and mitigate bias can help reduce its prevalence in generated content.

When harmful content does arise—be it through inadvertent generation by an AI model like ChatGPT or through user manipulation—it is essential for platforms hosting such technology to have robust reporting mechanisms and moderation policies in place. These systems enable swift action against inappropriate material while upholding freedom of expression within reasonable bounds.

Case studies from social media platforms illustrate both challenges and progress in this area. Platforms have struggled with moderating content at scale but have made strides by employing a combination of automated systems and human reviewers to address problematic posts effectively. Moreover, educating users on how to interact responsibly with AI- generated content is vital. Awareness campaigns can inform users about recognizing biased information and encourage critical thinking when engaging with such material.

In summary, addressing harmful or biased content requires a multifaceted strategy involving technological solutions for bias detection and mitigation; strong moderation policies; user education; and ongoing research into fairer algorithms—all aimed at fostering an online environment where constructive discourse thrives free from prejudice.

Privacy Concerns and Data Security

As we integrate ChatGPT into various aspects of our lives—from personal communication to business correspondence—the privacy concerns associated with its use become increasingly significant. Ensuring data security means protecting sensitive information from unauthorized access while respecting user privacy throughout interactions with the technology.

Data security involves safeguarding the infrastructure housing ChatGPT against cyber threats such as hacking attempts which could lead to data breaches exposing confidential information. Employing state-of-the-art encryption methods during data transmission ensures that even if intercepted by malicious actors, the information remains unintelligible.

On top of technical defenses against external threats lies the challenge posed by insider risks—whether intentional misuse by employees or accidental leaks due to negligence—which necessitates rigorous access controls within organizations using ChatGPT along with comprehensive employee training on data protection practices.

Privacy concerns extend beyond mere data protection; they encompass how collected information is utilized by companies behind these technologies. Transparency regarding data usage policies allows users to make informed decisions about engaging with services like ChatGPT while providing options for consent management empowers them over their personal information lifecycle—from collection through processing until deletion upon request according to applicable regulations like GDPR (General Data Protection Regulation).

Real-world incidents highlight why vigilance around privacy matters: The Cambridge Analytica scandal revealed how seemingly innocuous quiz apps could harvest vast amounts of Facebook user data without explicit consent leading not only public outcry but also increased regulatory scrutiny worldwide concerning digital privacy standards enforcement across tech industries including those developing conversational AIs such as OpenAI's GPT series products including GPT-3 upon which many versions are based today including this one you're interacting right now!

To conclude privacy concerns demand rigorous attention both technologically legally ensuring individuals retain control over their digital footprints even as they benefit from advancements offered artificial intelligence applications across different domains life work play!

Chapter 14: Safety Measures in Using ChatGPT

Mitigating Risks of Inappropriate or Offensive Content

The advent of conversational AI like ChatGPT has brought forth a myriad of opportunities for enhancing productivity and creativity across various fields. However, the potential for generating inappropriate or offensive content remains a significant concern. To mitigate these risks, it is essential to implement robust content moderation strategies that can preemptively identify and filter out such material.

One effective approach is the integration of advanced machine learning algorithms that are trained to recognize patterns associated with offensive language and themes. These algorithms can be continuously updated based on new data and evolving social standards to remain effective. Additionally, setting strict usage policies that clearly define unacceptable content types can guide users on what constitutes appropriate interactions with the AI.

User feedback plays a crucial role in refining these systems. Encouraging users to report instances where the AI fails to filter out inappropriate content helps developers understand the shortcomings of their moderation tools and improve them accordingly. Moreover, incorporating human oversight into the moderation process ensures an additional layer of scrutiny, especially for nuanced cases where context matters.

Real-world examples demonstrate the importance of these measures. For instance, Microsoft's chatbot Tay had to be taken offline within 24 hours due to its generation of offensive content after interacting with users who intentionally manipulated it. This highlights not only the need for strong initial safeguards but also for dynamic systems that can adapt to unexpected user behavior.

Reporting Issues Encountered during Use

When using sophisticated technologies like ChatGPT, encountering issues ranging from technical glitches to ethical concerns is inevitable. Establishing a clear and accessible reporting mechanism is vital for maintaining user trust and ensuring the safety and reliability of the platform.

Users should have multiple channels through which they can report problems—be it through in-app features, email support, or dedicated hotlines. These channels must be monitored by teams capable of addressing different types of issues promptly and effectively. For example, technical issues might require assistance from IT specialists, while content- related concerns might be best handled by moderators trained in ethical guidelines.

Transparency about how reports are handled reassures users that their concerns are taken seriously. Publishing regular transparency reports detailing the number and type of issues reported, as well as actions taken in response, fosters trust in the system's accountability mechanisms.

Case studies from platforms like Facebook illustrate both successes and challenges in this area. While Facebook has developed extensive reporting tools and publishes transparency reports regularly, it has also faced criticism over perceived inadequacies in handling reported issues swiftly or transparently enough.

OpenAI's Efforts towards User Safety

OpenAI recognizes that ensuring user safety is paramount when deploying AI models like ChatGPT into real-world applications. The organization undertakes several initiatives aimed at safeguarding users from potential harm while using their technology. One key effort is OpenAI's commitment to research into AI ethics and safety. By collaborating with academic institutions and other research organizations, OpenAI stays at the forefront of understanding how AI models interact with humans and societal norms—and how those interactions can be shaped positively.

Furthermore, OpenAI invests in developing more sophisticated content moderation tools specifically designed for conversational AI contexts. These tools are tailored to understand not just explicit language but also subtler forms of potentially harmful communication such as insinuations or manipulative dialogue patterns.

In addition to technological solutions, OpenAI engages with diverse communities including ethicists, policymakers, end-users, and advocacy groups—to ensure a wide range of perspectives inform their safety protocols. This inclusive approach helps anticipate complex ethical dilemmas before they arise.

Anecdotes from OpenAI's deployment practices provide insight into their proactive stance on user safety: When releasing newer versions of their models (like GPT-3), they often do so under controlled conditions initially— allowing select partners access under specific use-case agreements—to monitor how these models behave 'in the wild' before wider release.

In conclusion, each area—from mitigating risks associated with inappropriate content to reporting mechanisms and organizational efforts towards user safety—requires continuous attention as conversational AIs become increasingly integrated into our daily lives. Through vigilant application of advanced technologies coupled with human oversight; clear communication channels between users and developers; as well as ongoing research into ethical implications; we can strive towards creating an environment where conversational AIs serve us effectively without compromising our values or well-being.

Chapter 15: Understanding Limitations of ChatGPT

Incorrect or Nonsensical Responses

ChatGPT, like any other language model, is not immune to generating responses that are either incorrect or nonsensical. This limitation stems from the fact that the AI operates on patterns it has learned from its training data rather than a deep understanding of the world. When ChatGPT encounters questions or prompts that fall outside its training parameters or involve nuanced knowledge, it can produce answers that are factually wrong or logically incoherent.

One of the primary reasons for incorrect responses is the presence of gaps in ChatGPT's training data. Since it learns from a finite dataset, there may be topics or facts it is simply unaware of. For instance, if a user asks about a recent scientific discovery made after ChatGPT's last update, it might provide an outdated answer or guess based on related information it has been trained on.

Nonsensical responses often occur when ChatGPT fails to grasp the complexity of certain prompts. It might string together words and phrases that seem grammatically correct but lack meaningful content. For example, when asked to create a poem using highly technical jargon from quantum physics, ChatGPT might generate text that sounds poetic but makes little sense scientifically.

Another contributing factor to nonsensical outputs is the inherent randomness in AI's language generation process. To maintain fluency and variety in conversation, language models sometimes introduce randomness which can lead to unpredictable and illogical statements. Real-world implications of these limitations can be significant. In professional settings where accuracy is paramount—such as medical advice, legal consultation, or financial planning—relying on an AI-generated response without verification could lead to harmful decisions.

To mitigate these issues, users should always cross-check critical information provided by ChatGPT with authoritative sources. Developers are also working on improving AI models by expanding their datasets and refining their algorithms to reduce the frequency of incorrect and nonsensical responses.

Struggles with Understanding Context

Understanding context is crucial for any conversational agent aiming to provide relevant and coherent responses. However, ChatGPT often struggles with this aspect due to several inherent limitations in its design and function. The first challenge arises from the limited memory of conversational AI models like ChatGPT. They typically retain only a short history of previous interactions within a session which means they can lose track of earlier parts of a conversation as it progresses. This leads to situations where ChatGPT might give conflicting advice or repeat itself because it doesn't remember what was discussed several exchanges ago.

Moreover, context isn't just about remembering past interactions; it's also about grasping subtleties such as sarcasm, idiomatic expressions, cultural references, and personal nuances—all areas where ChatGPT can falter. The model may interpret sarcastic remarks literally or miss cultural cues that would significantly alter the meaning of a statement for human interlocutors.

Another dimension where context proves challenging for ChatGPT involves multi-turn dialogues where each response builds upon previous ones. In such scenarios, maintaining coherence over an extended interaction requires an intricate understanding of how different parts relate— a task that pushes current AI capabilities. In real-world applications like customer service chatbots or virtual assistants for scheduling meetings, these contextual misunderstandings can lead to frustration for users who expect human-like comprehension levels from AI systems.

To improve context understanding in conversational AI systems like ChatGPT:

1. Researchers are exploring ways to extend memory capabilities so they can reference more extensive conversation histories.

2. There's ongoing work on teaching models more about human social dynamics and communication subtleties.

3. Developers are incorporating feedback loops into interactions so users can correct misunderstandings immediate-

ly—helping the system learn in real-time.

Despite these efforts, achieving human-level contextual understanding remains one of the most challenging frontiers in artificial intelligence research today.

Difficulty in Providing Detailed Explanations

ChatGPT's ability to provide detailed explanations is another area where limitations become evident. While capable of generating fluent text across various topics and styles, when asked for depth—especially regarding complex subjects—the model may struggle significantly. This difficulty arises partly because providing detailed explanations requires not just surface-level knowledge but also an ability to draw connections between concepts and reason through them systematically—an area where machine learning models have yet to match human cognitive processes fully.

For example:

- In academic contexts involving deep expertise (like explaining advanced mathematical proofs), ChatGPT may offer general descriptions but fail at conveying intricate step-by-step reasoning.

- When discussing specialized fields such as medicine or law where precision is critical—and misinterpretations could have serious consequences—ChatGPT's explanations might lack necessary specificity or include inaccuracies due to its generalized training.

- In creative domains (like writing music critiques), while ChatGPT can mimic style convincingly enough at times; truly insightful analysis often requires subjective judgment informed by years of experience—a nuanced skill beyond current algorithmic capabilities.

These challenges highlight why detailed explanations remain largely domain-specific tasks best handled by experts within those fields rather than generalized AI systems like ChatGPT—at least until further advancements are made in machine learning techniques allowing deeper reasoning abilities akin to expert human thinkers.

To address this limitation:

1. There's ongoing research into developing more sophisticated natural

language processing algorithms capable of logical inference at higher levels.

1. Efforts are being made towards creating hybrid systems combining machine learning with rule-based reasoning—to leverage strengths from both approaches.

2. Specialized versions of conversational agents trained intensively on narrower domains show promise for better performance within those specific areas—but require substantial investment into targeted datasets and fine- tuning processes.

Until such improvements materialize broadly across conversational AIs landscape; users must temper expectations around depth-of-explanation capabilities while leveraging tools like ChatGPT—and continue relying on human expertise whenever detailed insights are essential.

Chapter 16: Making the Most of ChatGPT

Approaching Use with Caution and Critical Thinking

In the rapidly evolving landscape of artificial intelligence, ChatGPT stands out as a versatile tool capable of enhancing various aspects of work and creativity. However, its use must be approached with caution and critical thinking to avoid pitfalls associated with over-reliance on technology. Users should be aware that while ChatGPT can process and generate information at an impressive scale, it lacks human intuition and understanding. This means that while it can provide answers, those answers may not always be contextually appropriate or factually accurate.

Critical thinking is essential when interacting with ChatGPT. Users should question the validity of the information provided, cross-reference facts, and consider the source material that the AI might have been trained on. For instance, in scenarios where precision is paramount—such as legal advice or medical information—relying solely on ChatGPT could lead to erroneous conclusions. It's crucial to supplement AI-generated content with expert review.

Moreover, users should be cautious about potential biases in AI responses. Since ChatGPT learns from vast datasets that include human language from the internet, it may inadvertently reproduce biases present in those data sources. Users must critically assess whether the output perpetuates stereotypes or presents one-sided views and take steps to correct or balance such content.

Real-world examples highlight the importance of this approach: In healthcare, AI tools are used for diagnosis assistance but always under the supervision of medical professionals who ensure accuracy and ethical considerations are upheld. Similarly, in journalism, while automated systems can draft articles based on data inputs, editors ensure that reports maintain objectivity and factual integrity.

Understanding Capabilities for Maximum Benefit

To harness the full potential of ChatGPT for maximum benefit requires a deep understanding of its capabilities. Knowing what ChatGPT can do allows users to tailor their queries effectively and apply its strengths to suitable tasks while avoiding areas where it may fall short. ChatGPT excels at tasks involving natural language processing such as drafting text-based content for social media posts or business correspondence. Its ability to generate coherent narratives makes it an excellent tool for creating first drafts or brainstorming ideas which can then be refined by human creativity.

For example, marketers can leverage ChatGPT's writing capabilities to produce engaging content quickly but should then personalize these outputs before publication to ensure they align with brand voice and strategy. Similarly, programmers might use ChatGPT to write boilerplate code or debug simple issues; however complex programming challenges still require human expertise due to nuances in logic that AI might not grasp fully.

Another area where ChatGPT shines is education; personalized learning experiences become possible as it adapts responses based on user interaction history. Students struggling with specific concepts can receive tailored explanations which could lead to improved educational outcomes. However, understanding limitations is equally important as recognizing strengths. For instance, despite being a powerful tool for generating ideas in research settings, ChatGPT cannot replace domain-specific knowledge experts bring nor understand nuances within specialized fields without guidance.

Ensuring Ethical Practices while Using AI Technology

Ethical practices are paramount when integrating AI technologies like ChatGPT into daily operations across various sectors including education, research, legal advice among others. Ensuring responsible use involves several key considerations: respecting privacy rights; preventing misuse leading towards harmful consequences; maintaining transparency around how AI-generated content is used; combating biases within generated outputs; safeguarding against misinformation dissemination.

Privacy concerns arise when personal data is inputted into chatbots like ChatGPT since there's potential for misuse if sensitive information isn't handled properly by both OpenAI's systems and end-users themselves who must adhere strictly towards data protection regulations such as GDPR (General Data Protection Regulation).

Misuse prevention entails setting clear boundaries regarding acceptable uses of technology so as not promote unethical behavior—for example using chatbots unethically for impersonation purposes on-

line which could lead towards deception or fraudulence activities being carried out unknowingly by unsuspecting individuals.

Chapter 17: Applying ChatGPT in Customer Service

Enhancing Customer Support with ChatGPT

In the realm of customer service, the integration of AI-powered tools like ChatGPT can revolutionize how businesses interact with their customers. By leveraging the capabilities of ChatGPT, companies can offer more efficient, consistent, and personalized support to their clientele. One of the most significant enhancements is the ability to provide instant responses to customer inquiries. Unlike human agents who need breaks and have shift timings, ChatGPT can operate around the clock, ensuring that customers receive immediate assistance at any time.

Moreover, ChatGPT's advanced natural language processing allows it to understand and respond to a wide range of queries with human-like nuance. This capability enables it to handle complex customer service scenarios where context and tone are crucial. For instance, in situations where a customer is frustrated due to a defective product or delayed service, ChatGPT can be programmed to recognize emotional cues and respond empathetically while offering practical solutions.

Another area where ChatGPT enhances customer support is through its ability to learn from interactions and improve over time. By analyzing past conversations, it can identify patterns in customer issues and adapt its responses for better future engagements. This continuous learning process not only refines the quality of support but also helps in anticipating common problems before they escalate.

Furthermore, integrating ChatGPT into omnichannel support systems ensures that customers have a seamless experience across various platforms such as email, chat, social media, or phone calls. The AI can sync information across channels so that customers don't have to repeat themselves when switching mediums—a frequent source of frustration in traditional customer service settings.

Real-world examples include banks using chatbots for handling routine transactions and inquiries about account balances or recent transactions without compromising security or personal touch. Retailers employ AI chatbots during high-traffic events like Black Friday sales to manage an influx of customer questions without increasing wait times significantly.

Streamlining Frequently Asked Questions using ChatGPT

Frequently Asked Questions (FAQs) sections are vital for providing quick answers to common queries on websites and platforms. However, static FAQ pages often fall short in addressing all user concerns due to their limited scope and inability to engage in dynamic conversation. Herein lies the potential for ChatGPT: transforming FAQs from a passive list into an interactive experience.

By incorporating ChatGPT into FAQ systems, businesses enable users to ask questions in natural language rather than searching through a list of pre- written answers. The AI analyzes each query's intent and provides specific information tailored to individual needs. This approach not only saves time for users but also reduces frustration associated with navigating through irrelevant content.

Additionally, streamlining FAQs using ChatGPT minimizes the workload on human agents by deflecting common questions that do not require personalized attention. Agents are then free to focus on more complex issues that necessitate human intervention—thereby optimizing resource allocation within customer service departments.

An example of this application could be seen in travel agencies where customers frequently ask about baggage policies or check-in procedures. A chatbot powered by ChatGPT could instantly provide accurate information based on current airline regulations without directing users away from their current interaction window.

Personalized Recommendations and Assistance through ChatGPT

The power of personalization cannot be overstated in today's market landscape where consumers expect services tailored specifically for them. With data-driven insights gathered from user interactions and preferences, ChatGPT can deliver highly personalized recommendations that resonate with individual customers' needs.

For instance, e-commerce platforms can use ChatGPT bots as virtual shopping assistants that suggest products based on browsing history or previous purchases—much like an attentive salesperson who remembers your tastes every time you visit a store. These recommendations are not just limited to products; they extend into services such as suggesting articles related to items viewed or offering troubleshooting advice based on past support tickets.

Chatbots equipped with recommendation algorithms enhance user engagement by creating unique experiences for each visitor—turning casual browsers into loyal customers through relevant suggestions that may lead them down new paths they hadn't considered before.

A case study highlighting this would be streaming services employing AI chatbots which analyze viewing habits and subsequently recommend shows or movies fitting viewers' established preferences—effectively keeping subscribers engaged while promoting content discovery within their vast libraries.

In conclusion, applying ChatGPT across these three areas—enhancing overall customer support efficiency; streamlining access to information via dynamic FAQs; providing personalized recommendations—can significantly elevate the quality of service provided by businesses while fostering deeper connections between brands and consumers through meaningful interactions facilitated by cutting-edge technology.

"Mastering ChatGPT for Success" is a comprehensive guide that explores the multifaceted applications of the AI language model, ChatGPT, across various business and educational domains. The book delves into how leveraging ChatGPT can significantly enhance productivity, creativity, and efficiency in professional settings.

The text begins by discussing the integration of ChatGPT into daily business operations, emphasizing its role in streamlining communication and strategic planning. It provides insights on how to utilize the

AI for crafting effective presentations, managing budgets, navigating taxation intricacies, and driving profitability. The book also highlights the transformative potential of making ChatGPT a quasi-business partner through its capabilities in drafting business correspondence and coding.

In the realm of social media, readers learn strategies for scripting engaging content and automating postings with ChatGPT's assistance. This extends to research activities where the AI aids in generating ideas, conducting literature reviews, and analyzing data. The educational sector benefits from ChatGPT's personalized feedback mechanisms which bolster teaching methodologies and student learning experiences. However, the author stresses ethical considerations throughout these applications—emphasizing responsible use to avoid biases or misinformation while being mindful of privacy concerns. For legal professionals, while acknowledging its utility in document drafting and preliminary advice, the book cautions against over-reliance on AI for authoritative legal decisions.

Finally, "Mastering ChatGPT for Success" addresses using Chat-GPT as a creative partner in writing books. It encourages authors to harness AI- generated ideas without compromising their unique voice and creativity. Overall, this book serves as an essential resource for individuals aiming to capitalize on AI technology responsibly while navigating its limitations with critical thinking. It underscores the importance of human oversight when integrating ChatGPT into various professional practices to ensure ethical standards are upheld.

Chapter 18: Conclusion

Recap of the Value of ChatGPT in Various Domains

ChatGPT has emerged as a transformative tool across multiple sectors, demonstrating its versatility and adaptability. In education, it serves as an interactive platform for students to refine their language skills and receive instant feedback on their queries. The personalized attention that ChatGPT can provide is akin to having a tutor available around the clock, which is particularly beneficial in environments where educational resources are scarce.

In the realm of business, ChatGPT's applications are manifold. It aids in strategic planning by offering insights derived from data analysis, thus enabling businesses to make informed decisions. For startups and established companies alike, budgeting and taxation processes have been streamlined through ChatGPT's ability to process financial information efficiently. Moreover, its role in enhancing profitability cannot be overstated; by automating routine tasks such as business correspondence, organizations can allocate human resources to more complex and creative endeavors.

The creative industries have also harnessed the power of ChatGPT. Visual designers utilize it to brainstorm ideas or generate initial drafts for their projects. Writers leverage its capabilities for ideation and even co- authorship, allowing them to break through writer's block or explore new narrative paths.

In coding and software development, ChatGPT acts as an assistant that can debug code or suggest alternative programming solutions. Its impact extends to social media management where it crafts engaging content and schedules posts, thereby maintaining a brand's online presence with minimal human intervention.

However impressive these applications may be, they only scratch the surface of what is possible with AI like ChatGPT. Real-world examples abound: law firms using AI assistance for drafting legal documents; researchers employing it for literature reviews; educators integrating it into curricula for enhanced learning experiences—each instance underscores the multifaceted value that ChatGPT brings to various domains.

Importance of User Awareness and Responsibility

As we integrate tools like ChatGPT into our daily lives and work-spaces, user awareness becomes paramount. Users must recognize not only the capabilities but also the limitations inherent within AI systems. Misinformation remains a significant concern; hence users should verify any data or suggestions provided by ChatGPT against credible sources before acting upon them.

Ethical considerations take center stage when discussing user re-sponsibility with AI technologies. There is an imperative need to en-sure that AI does not perpetuate biases or infringe upon privacy rights.

Educators utilizing ChatGPT must safeguard student data while fostering an environment where AI complements human instruction without replacing it entirely.

Moreover, users should be cognizant of how they interact with AI systems like ChatGPT—ensuring respectful communication even when faced with errors or nonsensical responses from the AI system. Reporting inappropriate content helps improve these systems' safety measures over time.

The responsibility extends beyond individual use cases; organizations implementing AI must establish ethical guidelines governing its use—a framework that ensures transparency in how data is collected and used while preventing misuse of technology.

Future Prospects of AI Technology

Looking ahead at the future prospects of AI technology like Chat-GPT reveals a landscape brimming with potential advancements yet fraught with challenges requiring careful navigation. One area ripe for growth is natural language processing (NLP), which will likely see improvements in understanding context and nuance within human language—a leap forward from current limitations where misinterpretations still occur.

AI could revolutionize healthcare by providing diagnostic support or personalized treatment plans based on patient data analysis—though this raises critical questions about privacy and security that must be addressed proactively. In education, we might witness a paradigm shift wherein adaptive learning platforms powered by AI cater to individual student needs—offering tailored educational experiences that could reshape traditional classroom settings altogether.

The integration of augmented reality (AR) with AI presents another frontier—imagine technicians receiving real-time guidance via

AR glasses powered by an intelligent assistant like ChatGPT during complex repairs or surgeries.

Yet these advancements come hand-in-hand with societal implications— the displacement of jobs due to automation being one such concern. As we forge ahead into this brave new world dominated by artificial intelligence, there will be an ongoing need for dialogue between technologists, policymakers, ethicists, and society at large—to ensure that as we harness these powerful tools for progress, we do so responsibly and equitably for all members of society.

www.ingramcontent.com/pod-product-compliance
Lightning Source LLC
Chambersburg PA
CBHW051809130726
47987CB00003B/1172